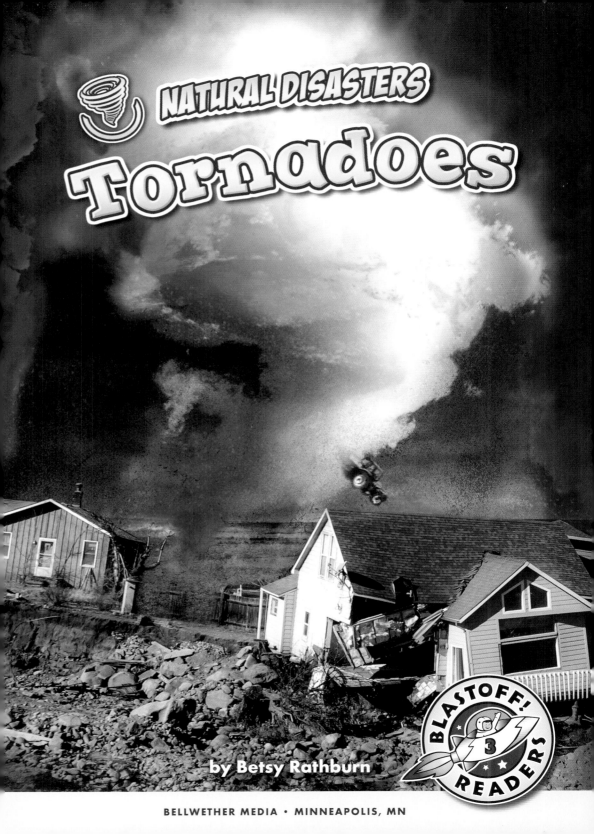

NATURAL DISASTERS

Tornadoes

by Betsy Rathburn

BLASTOFF! READERS

3

BELLWETHER MEDIA • MINNEAPOLIS, MN

Note to Librarians, Teachers, and Parents:

Blastoff! Readers are carefully developed by literacy experts and combine standards-based content with developmentally appropriate text.

Level 1 provides the most support through repetition of high-frequency words, light text, predictable sentence patterns, and strong visual support.

Level 2 offers early readers a bit more challenge through varied simple sentences, increased text load, and less repetition of high-frequency words.

Level 3 advances early-fluent readers toward fluency through increased text and concept load, less reliance on visuals, longer sentences, and more literary language.

Level 4 builds reading stamina by providing more text per page, increased use of punctuation, greater variation in sentence patterns, and increasingly challenging vocabulary.

Level 5 encourages children to move from "learning to read" to "reading to learn" by providing even more text, varied writing styles, and less familiar topics.

Whichever book is right for your reader, Blastoff! Readers are the perfect books to build confidence and encourage a love of reading that will last a lifetime!

This edition first published in 2020 by Bellwether Media, Inc.

Library of Congress Cataloging-in-Publication Data

Names: Rathburn, Betsy, author.
Title: Tornadoes / by Betsy Rathburn.
Description: Minneapolis, MN : Bellwether Media, Inc., 2020. | Series:
   Blastoff! Readers. Natural Disasters | Audience: Ages 5-8. | Audience: K
   to grade 3. | Includes bibliographical references and index.
Identifiers: LCCN 2019001489 (print) | LCCN 2019006065 (ebook) | ISBN
   9781618915689 (ebook) | ISBN 9781644870273 (hardcover : alk. paper) | ISBN
   9781618917485 (pbk. : alk. paper)
Subjects: LCSH: Tornadoes--Juvenile literature. | Natural disasters--Juvenile
   literature.
Classification: LCC QC955.2 (ebook) | LCC QC955.2 .R377 2020 (print) | DDC 551.55/3--dc23
LC record available at https://lccn.loc.gov/2019001489

Editor: Al Albertson   Designer: Josh Brink

Printed in the United States of America, North Mankato, MN

Table of Contents

What Are Tornadoes?

Tornadoes are storms made up of strong, swirling winds. Most tornadoes happen in an area of the United States called **Tornado Alley**.

But tornadoes can strike almost anywhere in the world!

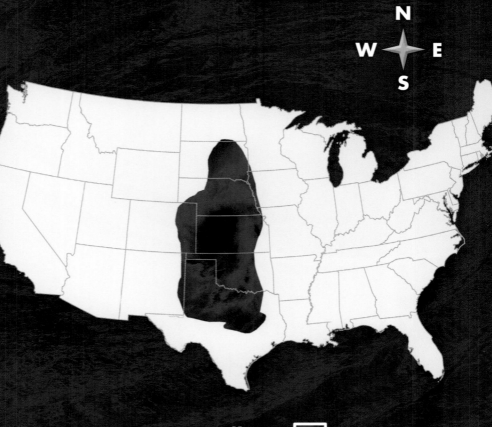

Tornado Alley

N
W E
S

Tornado Alley = ☐

How Do Tornadoes Form?

supercell

Most tornadoes form out of powerful thunderstorms called **supercells**. These storms have rotating **updrafts**.

Updrafts push wet, warm air up from the ground. This creates a swirling **vortex** in the clouds.

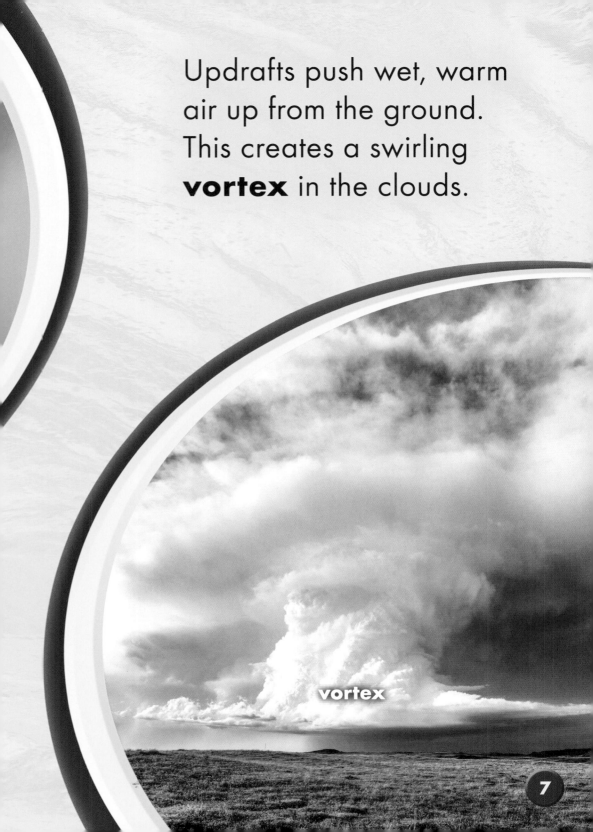

vortex

funnel cloud forming

When updrafts meet dry, cool **downdrafts**, funnel clouds may form. Then the vortex speeds up.

The funnel cloud is forced to the ground. It becomes a tornado!

How Tornadoes Form

cool downdrafts = →
warm updraft = →

Tornado Damage

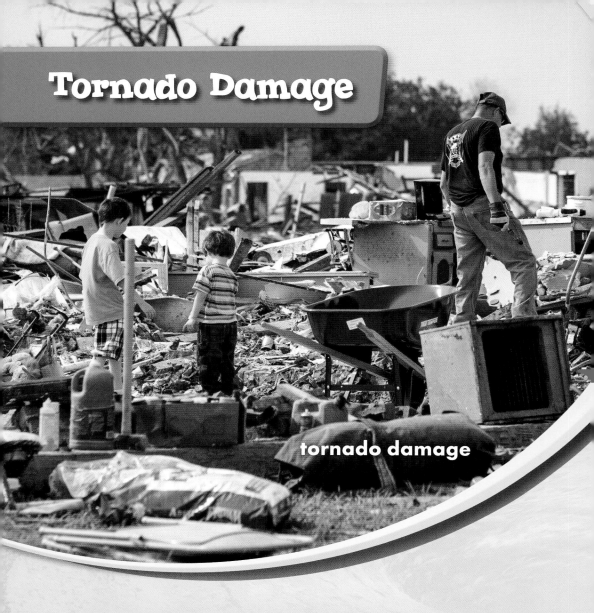

tornado damage

Tornadoes may last minutes or hours. Their winds may reach speeds over 300 miles (322 kilometers) per hour!

But tornadoes do not usually travel far. Most only cover about 6 miles (10 kilometers) before they end.

Powerful tornadoes cause a lot of damage. Their winds make flying **debris** deadly. Watch out!

power line

Tornado winds can also blow over power lines. This may force schools and businesses to close.

Tornado strength is measured by the **Enhanced Fujita Scale**. Strong tornadoes can destroy homes. They tear apart roofs and walls.

Mobile homes are especially at risk during tornadoes. People in them are not safe!

mobile home

Enhanced Fujita Scale

EF-0: winds 65 to 85 miles
(105 to 137 kilometers) per hour
- some broken branches
- sometimes no damage

EF-1: winds 86 to 110
(138 to 177 kilometers) per hour
- mobile homes flipped
- loss of doors and windows

EF-2: winds 111 to 135 miles
(179 to 217 kilometers) per hour
- roofs completely torn off houses
- mobile homes destroyed

EF-3: winds 136 to 165 miles
(219 to 266 kilometers) per hour
- trains flipped over
- serious damage to large buildings

EF-4: winds 166 to 200 miles
(267 to 322 kilometers) per hour
- entire houses completely destroyed
- large objects thrown

EF-5: winds more than 200 miles
(322 kilometers) per hour
- houses swept off foundations
- concrete buildings destroyed

Predicting Disaster

In the United States, tornadoes usually happen in spring. But they can strike at any time of year.

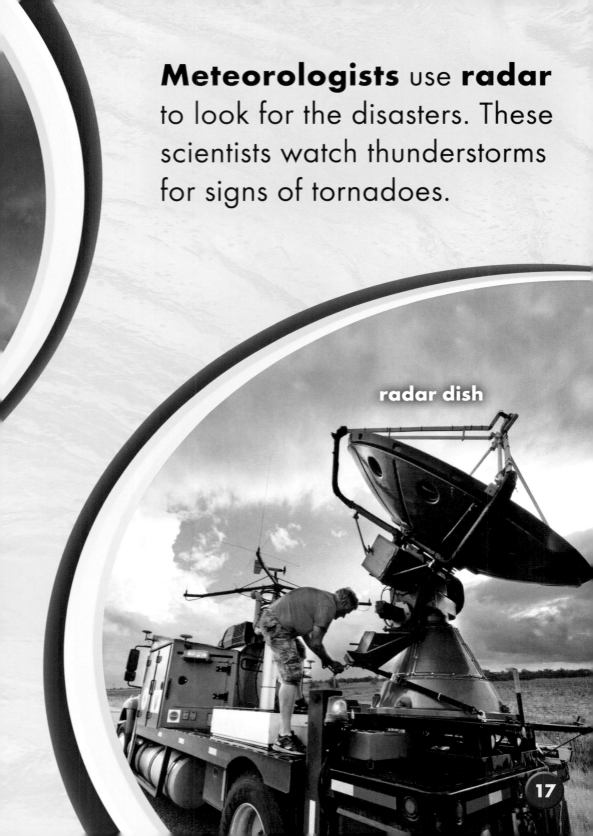

Meteorologists use **radar** to look for the disasters. These scientists watch thunderstorms for signs of tornadoes.

radar dish

17

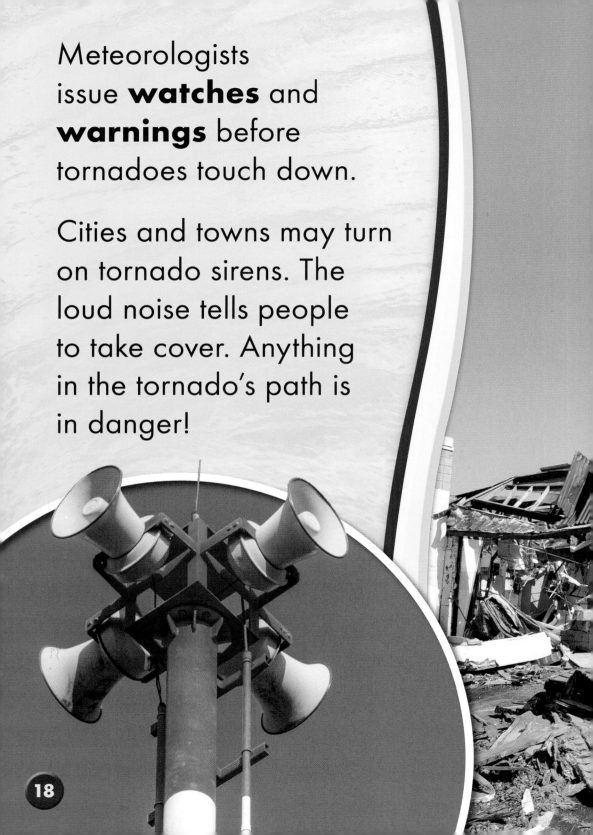

Meteorologists issue **watches** and **warnings** before tornadoes touch down.

Cities and towns may turn on tornado sirens. The loud noise tells people to take cover. Anything in the tornado's path is in danger!

Tornado Profile

Name:	2011 Joplin tornado
Dates:	May 22, 2011
Location:	Joplin, Missouri, and surrounding areas
EF Rating:	EF-5
Damage to Property:	• about 7,500 homes damaged or destroyed • about 550 businesses damaged or destroyed • around $3 billion in damage
Damage to People:	• 161 lives lost • 5,000 people lost work • 180 people moved from hospital

2011 Joplin tornado damage

During tornadoes, it is best
to stay indoors in basements
or away from windows.

People outside should stay away from power lines and trees. It is safer to lie flat in a field or ditch. Tornadoes cannot be stopped!

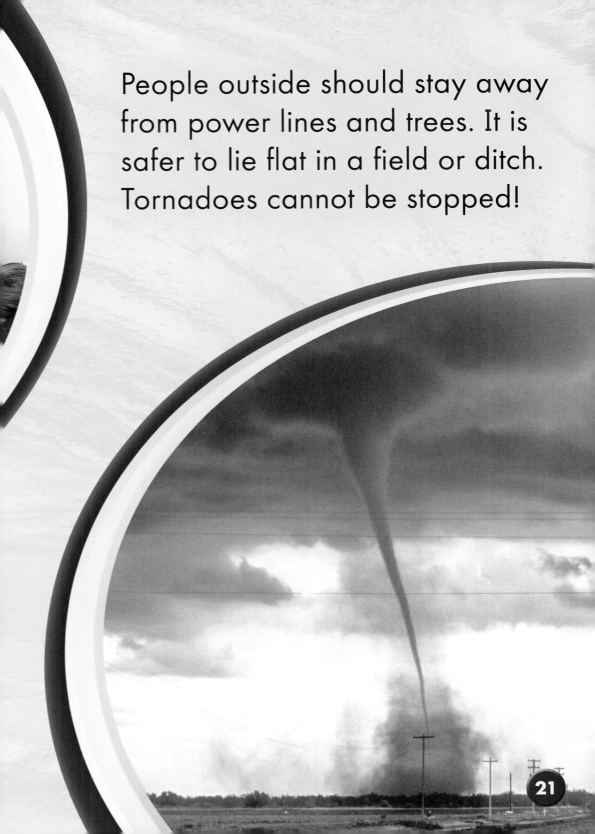

Glossary

debris—the remains of something broken down or destroyed

downdrafts—streams of cool, dry air that flow down during a tornado

Enhanced Fujita Scale—a scale used to measure tornado strength from EF-0 to EF-5

meteorologists—scientists who study weather

mobile homes—trailers that are used as houses at a permanent site

radar—a system that measures direction, distance, and speed; radar can track storms.

supercells—large thunderstorms that may produce tornadoes

Tornado Alley—an area in the central United States with a high number of tornadoes each year; Tornado Alley covers an area from Texas to South Dakota.

updrafts—streams of warm, moist air that flow up during a tornado

vortex—the central rotating part of a tornado

warnings—alerts issued by meteorologists when tornadoes have been spotted in an area

watches—alerts issued by meteorologists when thunderstorms may produce tornadoes

To Learn More

AT THE LIBRARY

Bowman, Chris. *Survive a Tornado.* Minneapolis, Minn.: Bellwether Media, 2017.

Murray, Julie. *Tornadoes.* Minneapolis, Minn.: Abdo Zoom, 2018.

Stoltman, Joan. *Following Extreme Weather with a Storm Chaser.* New York, N.Y.: Gareth Stevens Publishing, 2019.

ON THE WEB

Factsurfer.com gives you a safe, fun way to find more information.

1. Go to www.factsurfer.com.

2. Enter "tornadoes" into the search box and click 🔍.

3. Select your book cover to see a list of related web sites.

Index

The images in this book are reproduced through the courtesy of: Fer Gregory, cover (hero), Trong Nguyen,
cover (buildings), Cammie Czuchnicki, pp. 2-3, 11; Minerva Studio, pp. 4, 6; Image Source, p. 7; Jon Bilous/
Alamy, p. 8; trgrowth, p. 9; Newtonian, p. 10; Ryan McGinnis/ Alamy, pp. 12, 17; ungvar, p. 13; Alexey
Stiop, p. 14; Newtonian, p. 15; Mike Hollingshead/ Alamy, p. 16; forest71, p. 18; FEMA/ Alamy, p. 19; Larry
Fisher/ Alamy, p. 20; Menno van der Haven, p. 21.